Science and Engineering Practices

USING MODELS
AND MATH IN SCIENCE

by Riley Flynn

CAPSTONE PRESS
a capstone imprint

Pebble Plus is published by Capstone Press,
1710 Roe Crest Drive, North Mankato, Minnesota 56003
www.mycapstone.com

Library of Congress Cataloging-in-Publication Data
Cataloging-in-Publication data is on file with the Library of Congress.
ISBN 978-1-5157-0950-3 (library binding)
ISBN 978-1-5157-0982-4 (paperback)
ISBN 978-1-5157-1117-9 (eBook PDF)

Editorial Credits
Anna Butzer, editor; Sarah Bennett, designer; Eric Gohl, media researcher; Laura Manthe, production specialist

Photo Credits
iStockphoto: busypix, 5; Shutterstock: conrado, 11, bluehand, 9, marybethcharles, 20, Paul Aniszewski, 17,
Pavel L Photo and Video, 7, PhotoUG, 13, Tonello Photography, 19, Vladimir Wrangel, 15, wavebreakmedia,
cover

Design Elements: Shutterstock

Note to Parents and Teachers

The Science and Engineering Practices set supports Next Generation Science Standards
related to Science and Engineering Practices. This book describes and illustrates using
models and math in science. The images support early readers in understanding the text.
The repetition of words and phrases helps early readers learn new words. This book also
introduces early readers to subject-specific vocabulary words, which are defined in the
Glossary section. Early readers may need assistance to read some words and to use the
Table of Contents, Glossary, Read More, Internet Sites, Critical Thinking Using the Common
Core, and Index sections of the book.

Printed and bound in the United States of America.
11041R

Table of Contents

What Is a Model?

Do not be afraid! That is not a real volcano. It is a model of a volcano. Models look like real objects or events. They help us understand how things work.

Models also help us solve problems. A model of a car has a problem. Someone looks at the problem and fixes it. They build a real car that works.

Kinds of Models

Some models show small or
large copies of something.
A globe is a small model of
Earth. A solar system model shows
the planets that circle the Sun.

Other models help us test objects. Engineers use crash tests to see how their car designs handle crashes. These tests are models that show if cars are safe.

Using Math

Math is also used to model and describe things. Math shows us how to use numbers. We use numbers to count and measure. Numbers can show us patterns.

At the zoo you see two camels.
One has one hump. The other
has two humps. You can describe
a camel by the number of humps
it has.

Finding Patterns

Patterns repeat the order of things. Patterns are all around us. Look at a spider web. Do you see a pattern?

Look at the rings in a tree stump. Do you see a pattern? You can discover the age of a tree by counting these rings. Each ring equals one year.

Using Models

What type of house can best survive a hurricane or flood?

What You Need

- large, flat pan
- small blocks of wood
- small, smooth rocks
- rolling pin
- modeling clay
- plastic knife
- fan
- large pitcher of water

What You Do:

1. Build three houses on the pan. Each house should be the same height. Use the wood blocks to build the first house.

2. Build the second house out of rocks.

3. Roll out the modeling clay. Then cut it into small rectangles. Build the third house out of modeling clay.

4. Place a fan in front of the houses. Turn it on low. Did any of the houses fall?

5. Turn the fan on medium. Observe.

6. Turn the fan on high. Now did any houses fall? Which house stood the longest?

7. Repeat steps 1–3. Pour water into the pan. Did any of the houses collapse?

What Do You Think?

Make a claim. A claim is something you believe to be true. How did testing different models of houses help you learn?

Glossary

describe—to tell about something

engineer—a person who uses science and math to plan, design, or build

equal—the same as something else in size, number, or value

measure—to find out the size or strength of something

model—a representation to show the construction or appearance of something

pattern—a repeating arrangement of colors and shapes

Read More

Johnson, Robin. *Model It!* Science Sleuths. New York: Crabtree Publishing Company, 2015.

Miller, Reagan. *Engineers Build Models.* Engineering Close-Up. New York: Crabtree Publishing Company, 2014.

Internet Sites

FactHound offers a safe, fun way to find Internet sites related to this book. All of the sites on FactHound have been researched by our staff.

Here's all you do:
Visit www.facthound.com
Type in this code: 9781515709503

 Check out projects, games and lots more at
www.capstonekids.com

Critical Thinking Using the Common Core

1. Look at pages 17 and 19. Can you think of other places you have seen patterns? (Integration of Knowledge and Ideas)

2. Describe two ways scientists and engineers use models. (Key Ideas and Details)

Index